Baseball Facts & Fun Activity Book

Tony J. Tallarico

Batting is considered one of the most difficult feats in sports. A batter must try to hit a small round ball (traveling very fast) with a thin round bat!

Dover Publications, Inc.
Mineola, New York

If you're a baseball fan—or are simply interested in learning about America's "national pastime"—you will find plenty of fun in this fact-filled book. There are word-searches, mazes, codes, find-the-differences, and many other challenging puzzles. Learn when the first Major League Baseball night game was held, who was the first umpire, how much an official baseball weighs, and dozens of other fascinating facts! Are you ready for the first pitch? Let's get started!

Copyright

Copyright © 2010, 2017 by Tony J. Tallarico
All rights reserved.

Bibliographical Note

Baseball Facts & Fun Activity Book, first published by Dover Publications, Inc., in 2017, is a revised republication in a new format of *Baseball Activity Book,* originally published by Dover in 2010.

International Standard Book Number
ISBN-13: 978-0-486-81442-1
ISBN-10: 0-486-81442-4

Manufactured in the United States by LSC Communications
81442413
www.doverpublications.com

Emmett Littleton Ashford was a Major League umpire from 1966 to 1970. Unlike other umpires at the time, he exaggerated his calls with exciting gestures. What else was unique about Ashford?

A	C	E	F	I	M	N	P	R	S	T	U
11	4	9	2	7	12	6	3	8	1	5	10

HE WAS THE FIRST AFRICAN AMERICAN UMPIRE IN MAJOR LEAGUE BASEBALL.

Use the chart to decode the clues and complete this baseball fact.

Everyone knows that Babe Ruth was a home-run-hitting outfielder for the Yankees. But did you know that he started out on the Red Sox playing a very different position?

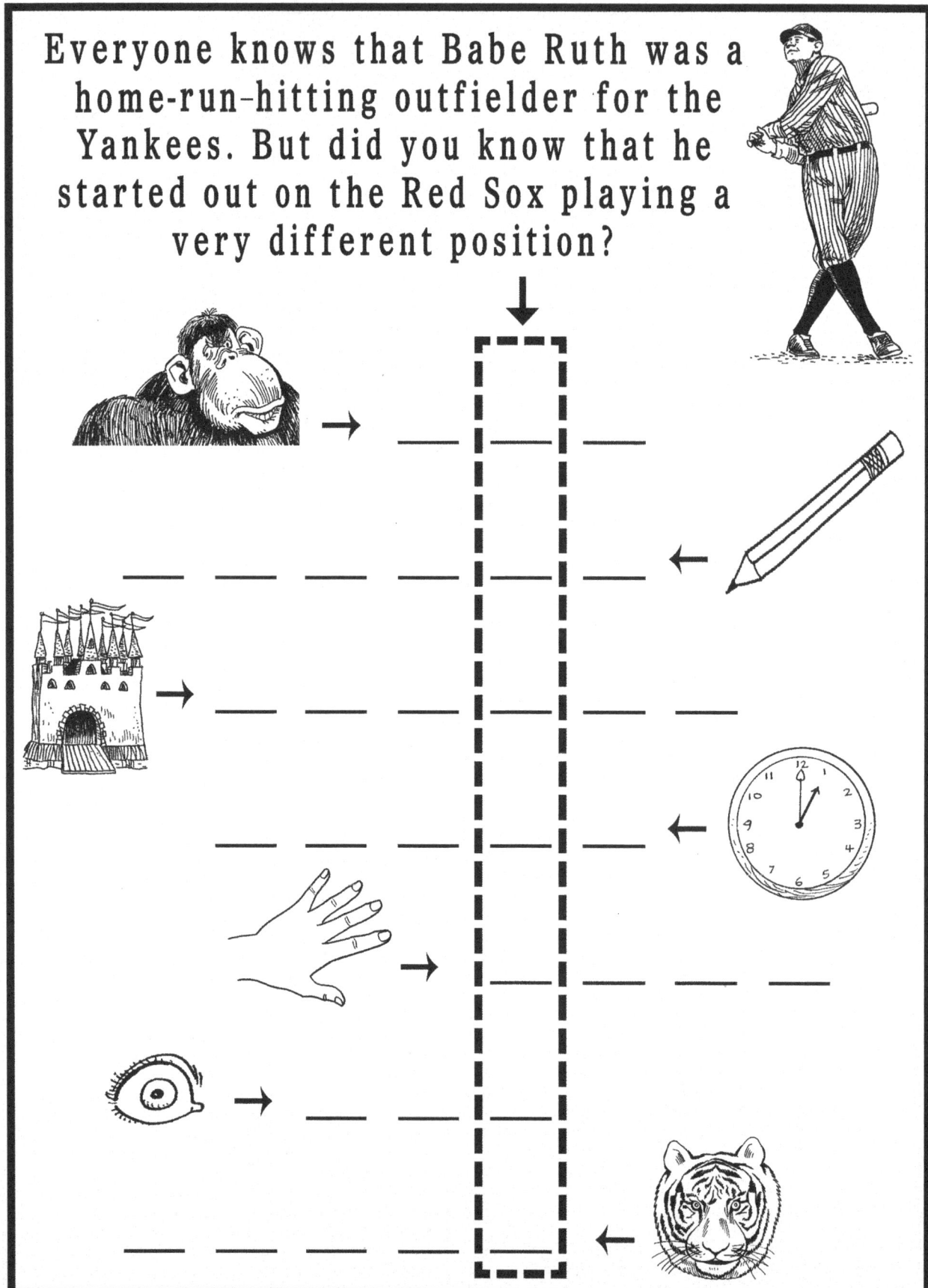

Write the name of each object pictured.
One letter from each word will help spell the hidden answer.

Although many believed at one time that Abner Doubleday invented baseball, it is today considered a myth by sports historians. This man is officially credited (by the U.S. Congress) with organizing the rules of the game.

A	L	I	E	X	O
A	H	N	T	D	E
S	R	C	A	R	O
A	T	W	R	U	M
I	G	B	H	E	T

ALEXANDER CARTWRIGHT

Circle only the letters that are in a box with a baseball. List those letters, in the order they appear, to spell the name of baseball's organizer.

The Little League was started in 1939 as a three-team league in Pennsylvania. Today more than 2 million kids participate in Little League worldwide!

- BATTER
- CATCH
- COACHES
- FAIR
- FUN
- LEARN
- PLAYERS
- PRACTICE
- RESPECT
- RULES
- SAFE
- SPIRIT
- TEACH
- TEAMS
- THROW
- TRY

```
B A T E R C
T S R E Y A L P
Y R T H E R O W
E P E F C A L O
C L A R S A L R
I S M B A T E H
T H S P I R I T
C O A C H E S C
A N D S E T H E
R U L E S T F P
P F H C T A C S
E C I L I B A E
L U N R A E L R
```

Find and circle the words, listed above, that have something to do with Little League.

A baseball is covered with two strips of white horsehide (or cowhide) tightly stitched together. Approximately how much does an official baseball weigh?

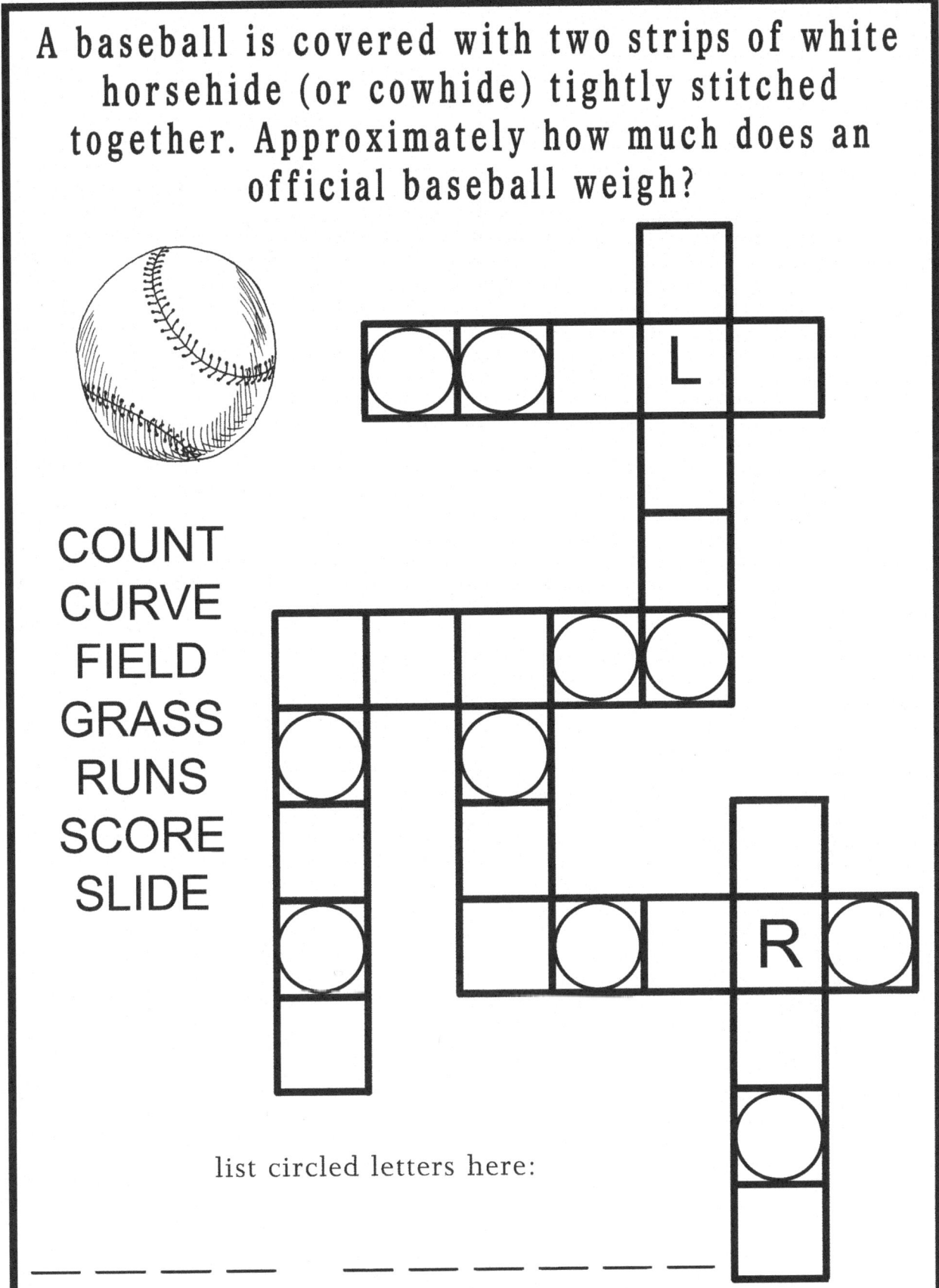

COUNT
CURVE
FIELD
GRASS
RUNS
SCORE
SLIDE

list circled letters here:

_____ _____

Write the baseball words, listed above, in the spaces where they belong in the puzzle. The circled letters, written in order, will spell the answer.

5

Although umpires aren't always a favorite of fans and players, they are an important part of the game. Umpiring goes back to 1876 when a man named William McLean became the first professional umpire. He umpired the very first game in National League history!

ANCHOR ☐   BASEBALLS ☐ ☐ ☐   BINOCULARS ☐   BOWLING BALL ☐
BROOM ☐   COFFEE POT ☐   EYEGLASSES ☐   STAR ☐

Find and circle the hidden objects in this cartoon.
Use the checklist to keep track.

"Take Me Out to the Ball Game" is an early 20th century song that has become the unofficial anthem of baseball. Usually sung during a game's 7th inning stretch, it was written by Jack Norworth and Albert Von Tilzer. What is strange about the song's authors?

__ __ __ __ __ __ __   __ __ __   __ __
O F J U I F S   P O F   P G

__ __ __ __   __ __ __ __ __ __ __ __
U I F N   B U U F O E F E

__   __ __ __ __   __ __ __ __ __
B   H B N F   C F G P S F

__ __ __ __ __ __ __   __ __ __
X S J U J O H   U I F

            __ __ __ __!
            T P O H

Write the alphabet letter that comes before each of the letters in the spaces above. Then read the baseball fact.

An error is when a fielder misplays a ball and allows a batter or baserunner to reach one or more bases. The picture below is full of errors!

Can you find and circle eleven things that are wrong, or just don't belong, in this baseball scene?

The first night game in Major League Baseball was played in May 1935. The Reds beat the Phillies 2-1 at a ballpark in Cincinnati, Ohio.

FIRST, _____, THIRD ▶ _ E _ _ _ D

OPPOSITE OF FAKE ▶ _ _ _ A _

FUNNY CIRCUS PERFORMER ▶ _ _ _ W _

FOUND ON THE BEACH ▶ _ _ _ D

A BABY COW, CAMEL OR MOOSE ▶ C _ _ _

WRITING TOOL THAT NEEDS SHARPENING ▶ _ _ N _ _ L

OPPOSITE OF OLD ▶ _ _ U _ _

To learn the name of the ballpark that hosted the first night game, complete the answers to the clues. One letter from each answer will help spell out the name.

9

The National Baseball Hall of Fame and Museum was first dedicated in 1939.

ARTIFACTS ☐ DISPLAY ☐ HISTORY ☐ HONOR ☐
INDUCTEES ☐ PRESERVE ☐ REPLICAS ☐ VISIT ☐

Find and circle the baseball words hidden in the puzzle.
The remaining letters, written in the blanks in the order they appear,
will spell the location of the Hall of Fame.

Batting is considered one of the most difficult feats in sports. A batter must try to hit a small round ball (traveling very fast) with a thin round bat!

Find and circle, in the picture on the right, nine things that are different between these two pictures of Hall of Famer Mickey Mantle.

This Hall of Fame second baseman was the first African American player in Major League Baseball.

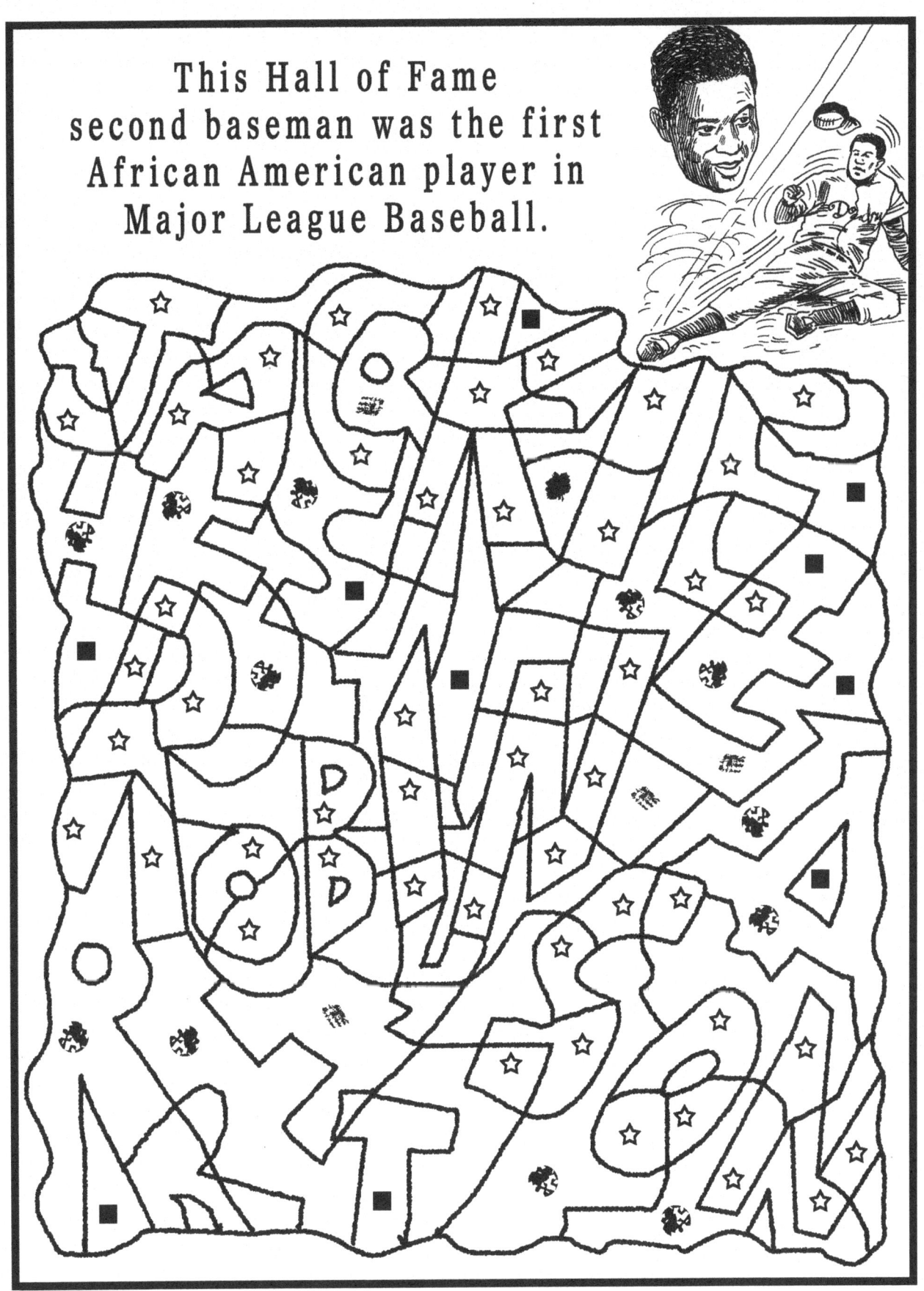

Use a pencil to shade the areas that contain a STAR, and you will reveal the name of this historic player.

Unlike other sports that use a clock, baseball isn't controlled by a specific length of time. A typical baseball game is played in 9 innings.

_ N F _ _ L D _ R
Shortstop or second baseman for example

C _ TCH _ R
Player who crouches behind home plate

_ MP _ R _
One of 4 officials on the field

TR _ PL _
When batter makes it safely to third base without stopping

B _ TT _ M
Second half of an inning

In the blanks, add the correct vowels to these baseball words. The clues can help you.

A women's professional baseball league existed from 1943 to 1954. The league had such teams as the Kenosha Comets, Racine Belles, and Rockford Peaches.

Use the chart to decode the name of the women's professional baseball league.

ALL-AMERICAN GIRLS PROFESSIONAL BASEBALL LEAGUE

Teams have used nicknames to identify themselves since the early days of baseball. One of the first recorded games took place between two teams simply called "New York" and "Knickerbockers."

```
T W I N S S T E M S
I R E O S R O Y A E
G O T B E S L A R I
E B U S L A K X L K
R C G L O M E T I C
S T N A I G T O N O
E V A B R A V E S R
T I G X O S D E R E
    R O Y A L S
```

BRAVES ☐ CUBS ☐ GIANTS ☐
MARLINS ☐ METS ☐ ORIOLES ☐
RED SOX ☐ ROCKIES ☐ ROYALS ☐
TIGERS ☐ TWINS ☐

Find and circle the names of these eleven teams in the puzzle.

The Little League World Series was first held back in August 1947 in Pennsylvania. No matter where in the world the teams are from, this World Series is always played yearly in Pennsylvania.

The letter "W" is hidden nine times in this picture. Find and circle each "W."

There are a few different throwing styles used by pitchers. The most common is an overhand delivery, but some pitchers use a sidearm or a submarine style delivery.

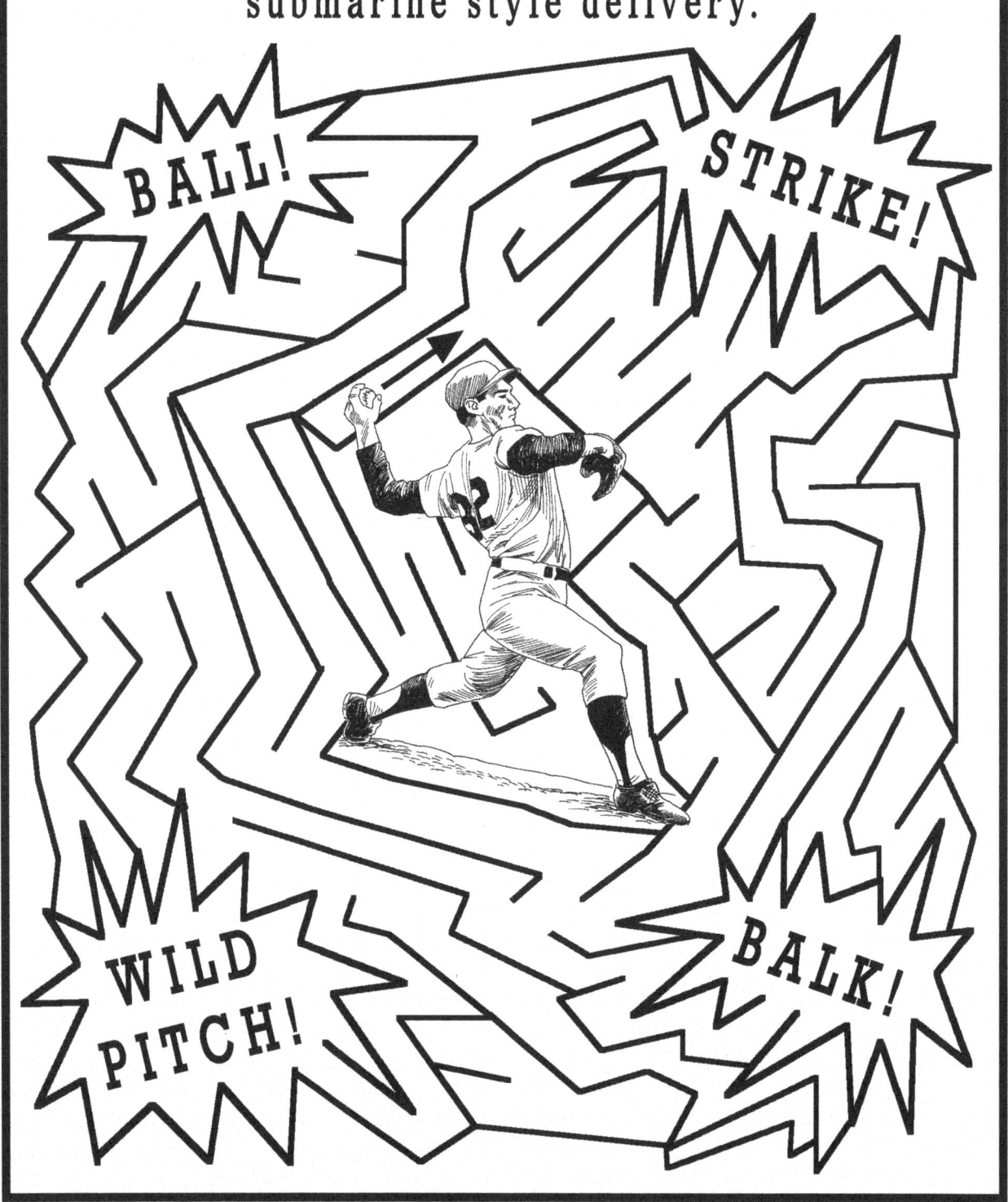

Help this pitcher throw only a strike by successfully traveling to the end of this maze.

While the exact origin of baseball is unknown, most historians think that it is based on a sport that began in Ireland.

Write the name of each object pictured. One letter from each word will help spell the name of this nineteenth-century sport.

19

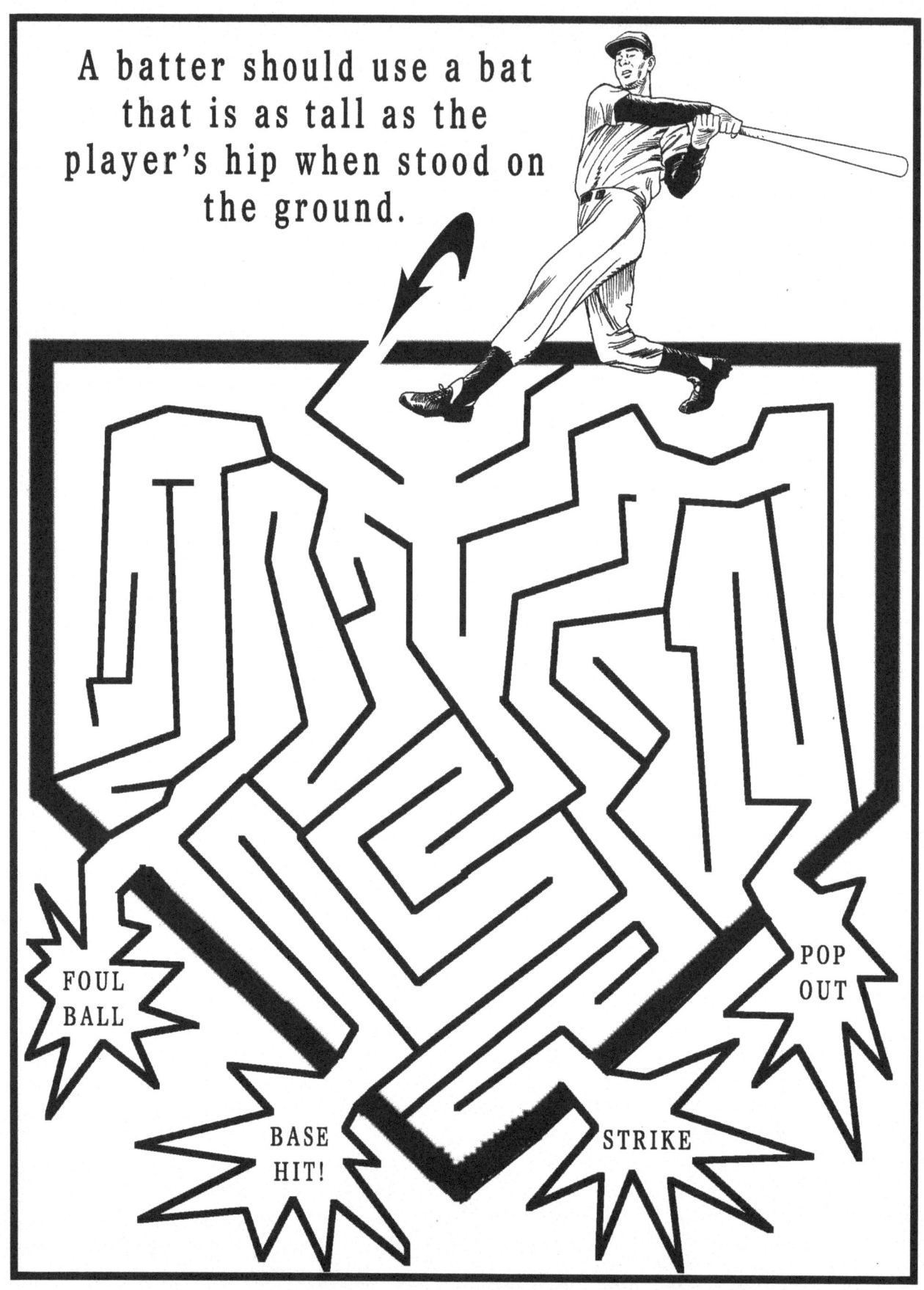

A batter should use a bat that is as tall as the player's hip when stood on the ground.

FOUL BALL

POP OUT

BASE HIT!

STRIKE

Help this batter get only a base hit by traveling through the maze.
Be careful—or you might hit a foul ball!

A pitch is the act of throwing a baseball toward home plate to start a play. Pitchers throw many different types of pitches.

CHANGEUP ❏ CURVEBALL ❏ CUTTER ❏ FASTBALL ❏ FORKBALL ❏ SCREWBALL ❏ SINKER ❏ SLIDER ❏

```
L L A B E V R U C
L L A B K R O F H
A R E T T U C E A
B E L L F S L K N
T D N G V B A L G
S I N K E R K S E
A L O U T E B V U
F S F B A L E U P
L L A B W E R C S
```

Can you find and circle the names of the types of pitches shown in the box above the puzzle?

21

Music is a common sound at sporting games - especially organ music at ballparks. The first organ debuted at a Major League ballpark in April 1941.

ROY NELSON AT WRIGLEY FIELD IN CHICAGO.

To find out who first played the organ at a Major League ballpark, cross out the letters that have a TRIANGLE.
Write the remaining letters in order in the blank spaces.

Major League Baseball has a rule that "no one except players, substitutes, managers, coaches, trainers, and batboys shall occupy the dugout during a game."

BASEBALL ☐ FISH ☐ FLYING BAT ☐ FOOTBALL ☐
HOCKEY PUCK ☐ HOURGLASS ☐ PALM TREE ☐ PIE ☐
SCISSORS ☐ SCREWDRIVER ☐

Find and circle the hidden objects in this cartoon.

The four infielders are the first baseman, second baseman, shortstop and third baseman.

A.

B.

C.

D.

E.

These infielders may look the same in every picture, but one is different from the others. Find and circle the infielder that is different.

Most team sports play on a rectangular field (like basketball and football). But baseball is played on a wedge-shaped field called a diamond.

Find and circle twelve things that are wrong, or don't belong, on this baseball field.

A stadium is a place where an indoor or outdoor game of baseball can be played.

**BASES
BULLPEN
DIAMOND
DUGOUT
ON DECK
SEATS**

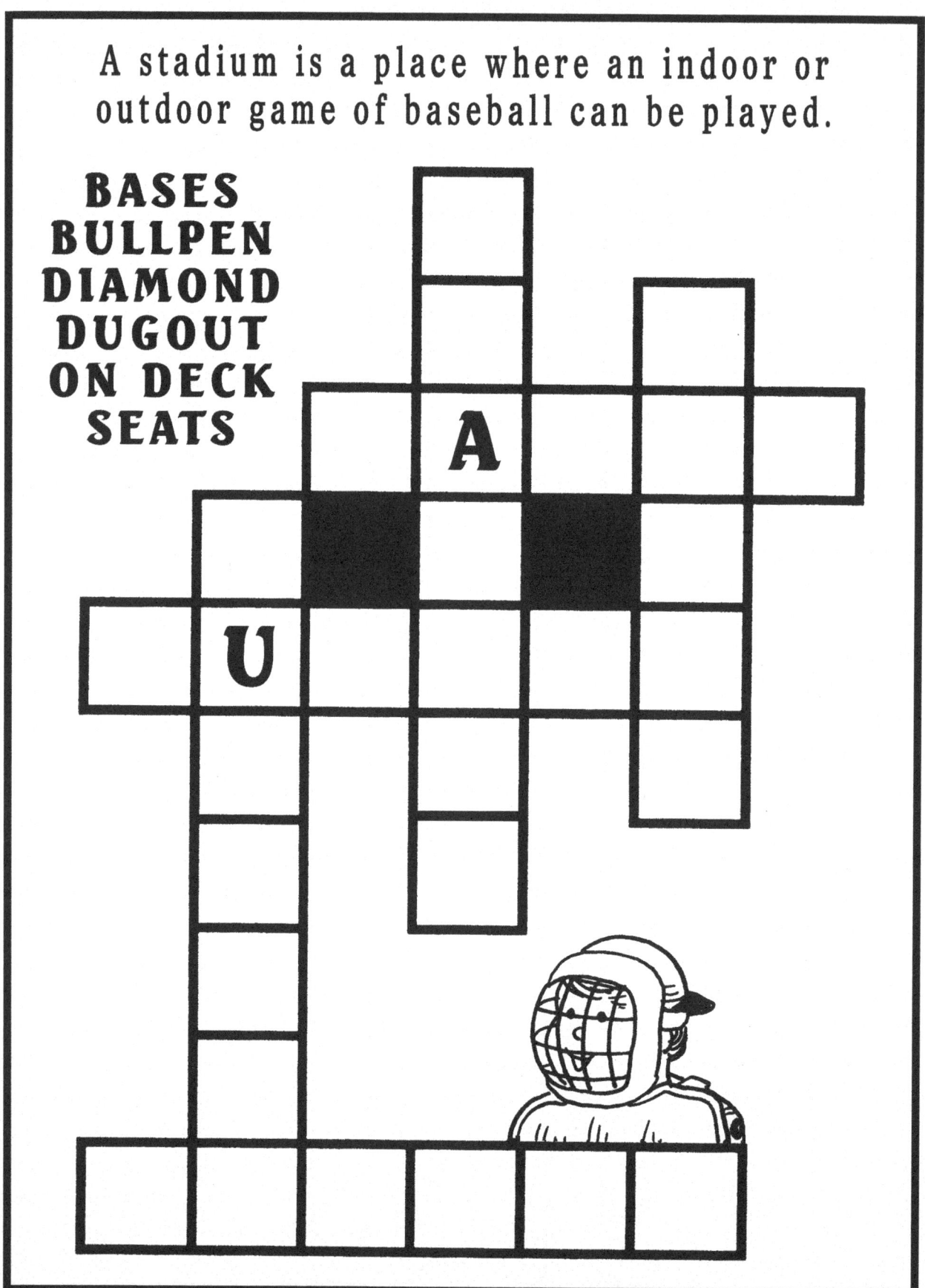

Write these words having to do with baseball stadiums in the correct spaces in the puzzle.

"B" is for baseball!

Find and circle fifteen things in this wacky baseball scene
that begin with the letter "B."

Some of the first baseball trading cards were made in the late 1860s by a sporting goods company. The cards were used to advertise their products.

Today, collecting cards is still a popular hobby among sports fans.

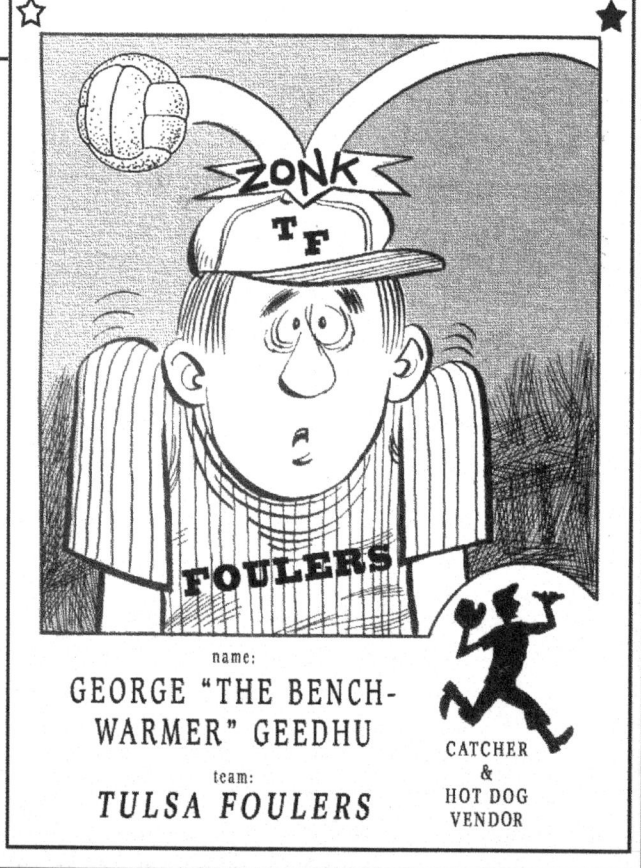

Can you find and circle eight things that are different between these two silly baseball cards?

WHO AM I?
"I'm a Hall of Famer who played my first Major League game in 1951 and my last in 1973. During those years I hit 660 home runs."

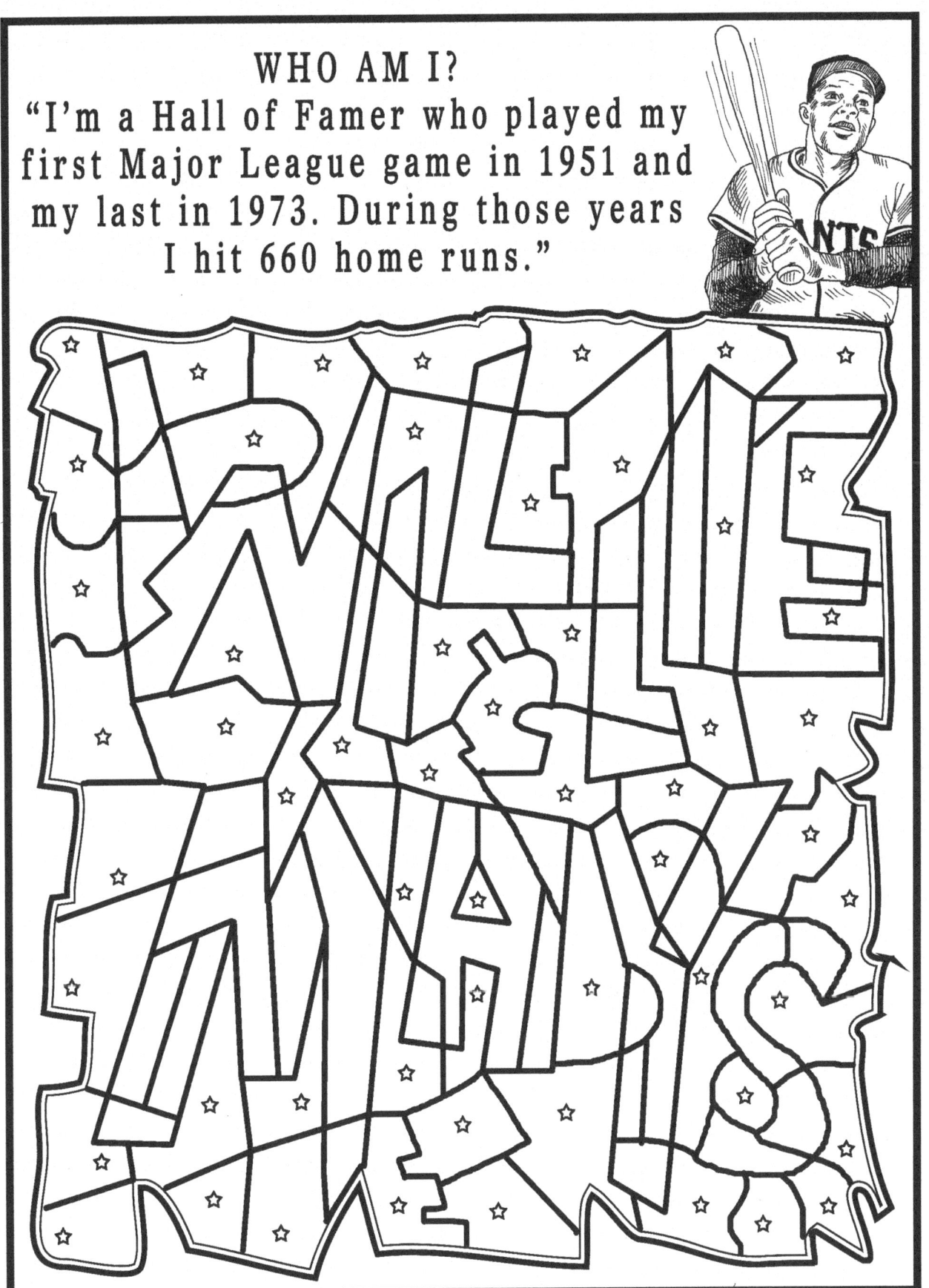

Use a pencil to shade the areas that contain a STAR, and you will reveal the name of this baseball superstar.

The first Major League All-Star game was played on July 6, 1933, in Chicago. The American League won over the National, 4-2.

M I S S I S S I _ P I

F _ O R I D A

U T _ H

W _ O M I N G

A L A _ A M A

I D _ H O

D E _ A W A R E

I L _ I N O I S

In this list of the names of eight U.S. states, each state is missing a letter. Fill in each name and then read down the starred column to discover a familiar phrase.

It wasn't always "three strikes and you're out!" In 1886 the number of strikes required for a strikeout was four.

TOTAL: ____

How many times does the word STRIKEOUT appear in this puzzle?
Find and circle each one.

In order to throw a baseball accurately, your fingers should be placed over the top of the seams. This will give you a good grip.

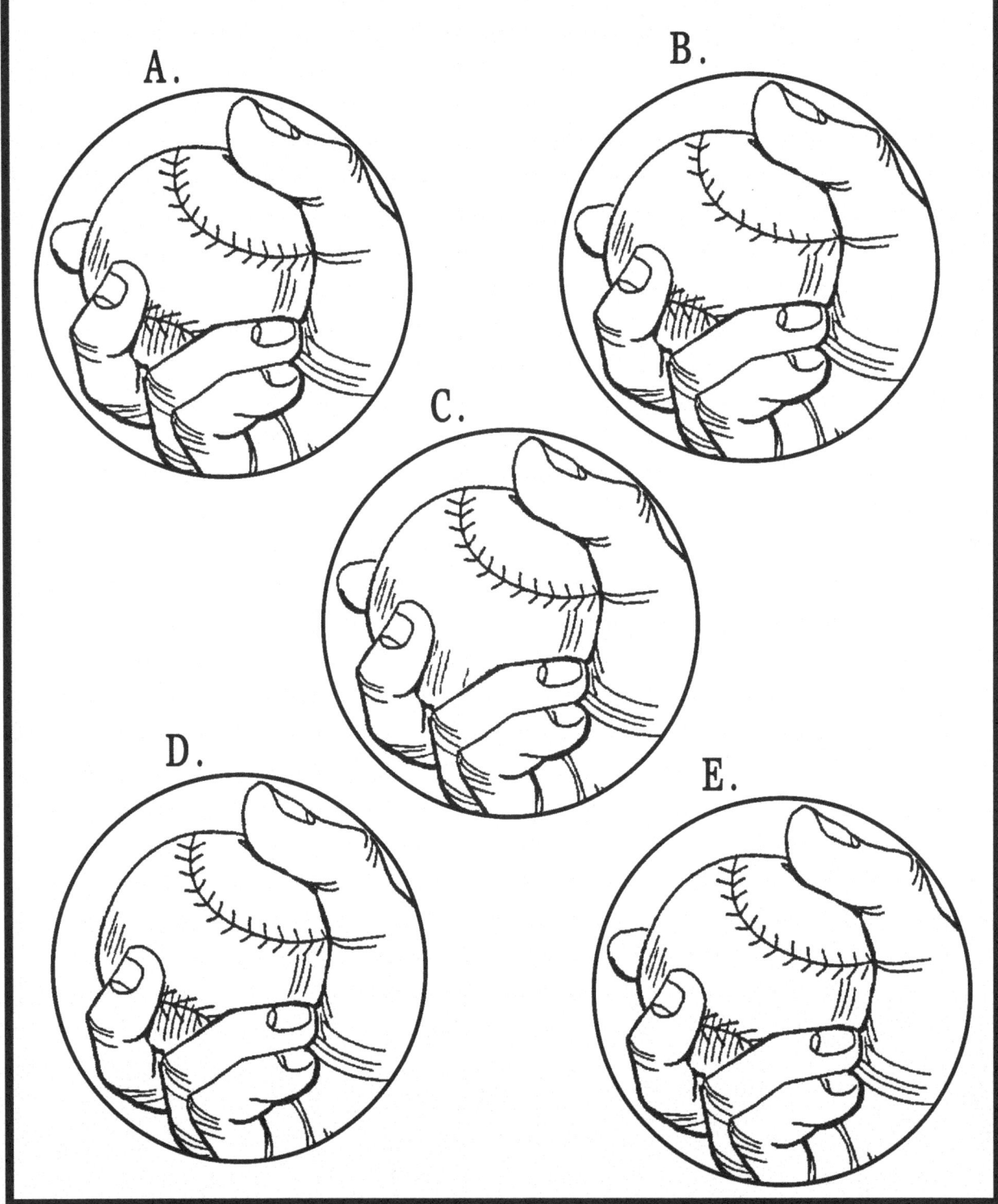

Two of the pictures are exactly the same. Find and circle them.

Every U.S. President since William Howard Taft has thrown out at least one ceremonial first ball or pitch, either for Opening Day, the All-Star Game, or the World Series. President Taft started the tradition on Opening Day in 1910 at Griffith Stadium, Washington, D.C.

Here are two pictures of President Taft.
Find and circle six things in picture #2 that are different from picture #1.

In 1939, Yankee Lou Gehrig became the first player in baseball to have his uniform number retired.

Use a pencil to shade the areas that contain only a BASEBALL to reveal Gehrig's uniform number.

Do you have a favorite baseball player?

BONDS
CLEMENS
COOK
GARCIA
GLAVINE
HOWARD
JETER
JONES
LEE
MARTINEZ
ORTIZ
RAMIREZ
RIVERA
RODRIGUEZ
SANTANA
WEBB
WRIGHT

Find and circle the names of these baseball players in the puzzle.

The Cy Young Award is given each year to the best pitchers in Major League Baseball, one each for the American and National leagues. The award is in honor of Hall of Fame pitcher Cy Young.

```
K O U F A X C
R H C O N E A
E Y N R S V R
V R D D W B L
A R E L Y L T
E E X A N U O
S P A H N E N
```

BLUE
CARLTON
CONE
FORD
KOUFAX
LYLE
PERRY
SEAVER
SPAHN
WYNN

Can you find the names of these Cy Young winners in the puzzle? Circle the names as you find them.

"Rainout," "rain delay" and "rain stopped play" are terms used when wet weather affects a baseball game.

In each blank, write the alphabet letter that comes before each letter. Then read a statement about baseball and the weather.

The distance a baseball travels when hit depends on the angle at which the ball leaves the bat and how fast the ball is hit. What is a hard-hitting batter in baseball often called?

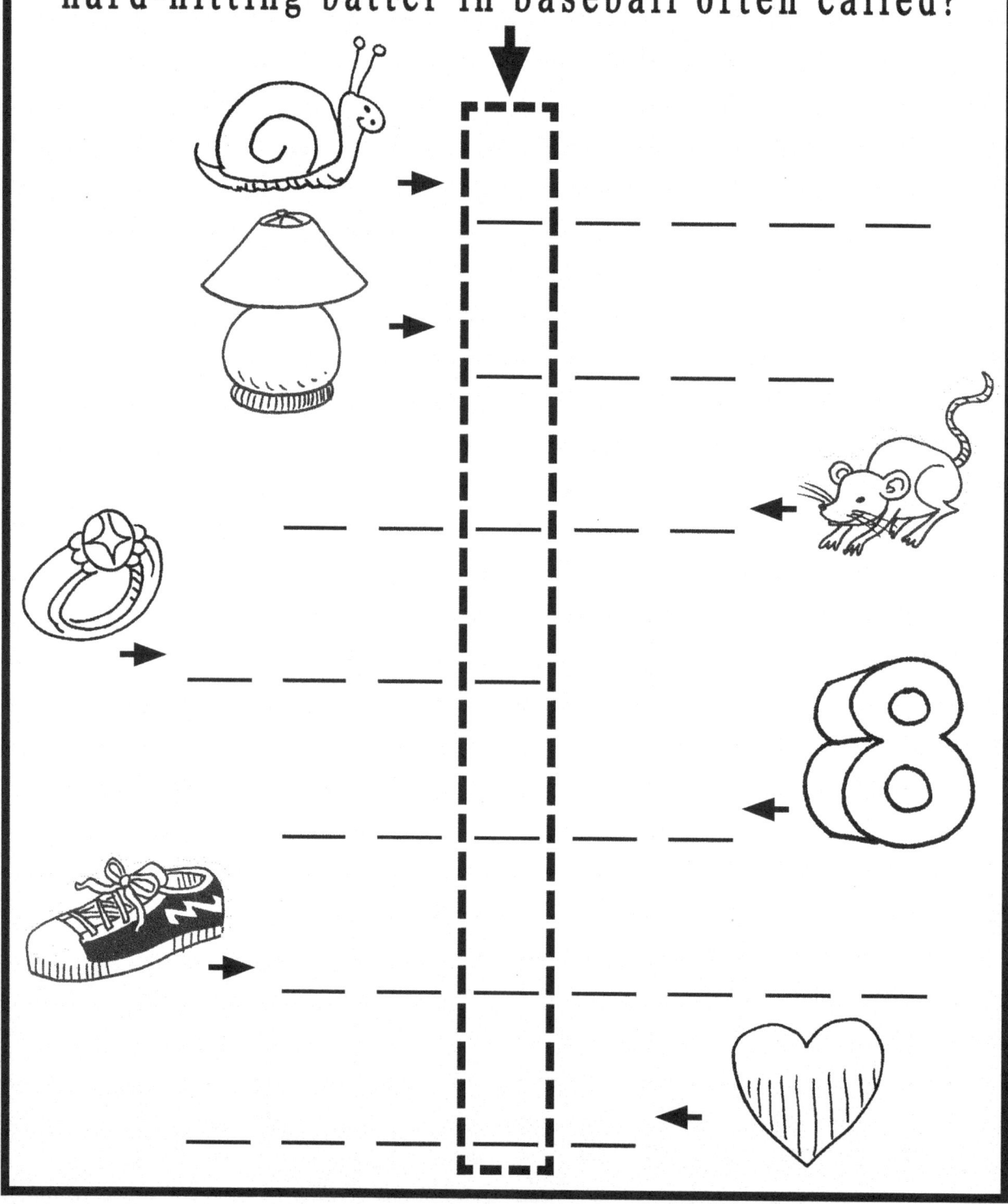

Write the name of each object pictured.
One letter from each word will help spell the answer.

Where in the U.S. was game 1 of the very first World Series played in 1903?

Complete this maze to find the correct answer.

39

SOLUTIONS

Page 1

Page 2

Page 3

Page 4

Page 5

Page 6

Page 7

Page 8

Page 9

Page 10

Page 11

Page 12

Page 13

Page 14

Page 15

Page 16

Page 17

Page 18

Page 19

Page 20

Page 21

Page 22

Page 23

Page 24

Page 25

Page 26

Page 27

Page 28

Page 29

Page 30

Page 31

Page 32

Page 33

Page 34

Page 35

Page 36

Page 37

Page 38

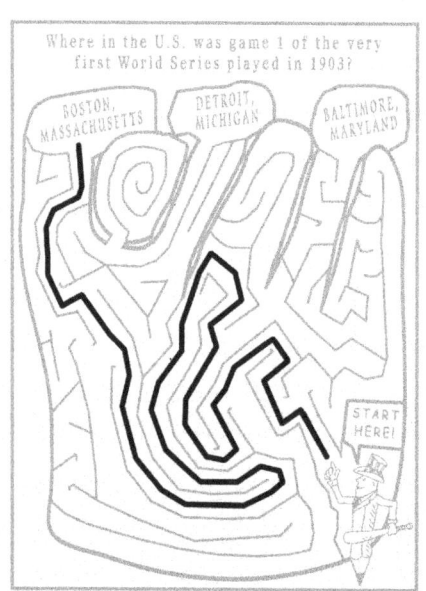

Page 39